Walking Past Midnight

)

Alabama Poetry Series

General Editors: Chase Twichell and
Thomas Rabbitt

Walking Past Midnight

John Morgan

The University of Alabama Press
Tuscaloosa and London

Copyright © 1989 by
The University of Alabama Press
Tuscaloosa, Alabama 35487
Manufactured in the United States of America

Library of Congress Cataloging-in-Publication Data

Morgan, John, 1943–
        Walking past midnight / John Morgan
            p.   cm. — (Alabama Poetry Series)
        ISBN 0-8173-0431-2 (alk. paper). —
        ISBN 0-8173-0432-0 (pbk. : alk. paper)
        I. Title.   II. Series.
        PS3563.0863W35   1989
        811'.54—dc19   88-34009   CIP

British Library Cataloguing-in-Publication Data available

For Nancy,
Jeffrey, and
Benjamin

Acknowledgments

Some of the poems in this collection appeared originally in the following journals and chapbooks:

The American Poetry Review: "The Inside Passage"
Antaeus: "Letter from the Camp: The Pearl Fishers"
Chelsea: "A Dirt Road West of Fairbanks"
Denver Quarterly: "The Siege of Leningrad, 1941-42,"
        "The Wreck"
Dooryard Press: "The Cyclist" (chapbook)
Harvard Magazine: "Pictures of the Dead"
Image: "Moo"
The Kenyon Review: "The Third Walk: McKinley Park Hotel . . .,"
        "Walking Past Midnight"
Montana Review: "Crossing the Rhine," "To the Muse"
The North American Review: "Married," "The Beach
        Walk at Port Townsend, WA"
Owl Creek Press: "The Inside Passage," "Osteology of the Ants,"
        "USS *Argonaut*," "Rembrandt on the Hudson" (chapbook,
        titled *The Inside Passage*)
Permafrost: "Rembrandt on the Hudson"
Poetry (Chicago): "USS *Argonaut*"
Poetry Northwest: "Osteology of the Ants"
The Yale Review: "The Suppressed"

Contents

I

The Siege of Leningrad, 1941-42

How boring at seventeen to have
responsibilities! My little
brother plays with boxes. Mother
and Aunt lie in the cold
back room too heavy to move.
I keep it closed because I know a rat
has visited their faces.

Last June when our German friends
decided to pay a call, I curled
at my rooftop post like
a cat staring into a bowl.
The blimps overhead were strange
white fish. In the light
that crept across the pole,

my friends and I read Pushkin.
At times it felt like me
drifting over the streets,
each roof, each silvery spire
in the midnight glow engraving
a past that was
learning to slowly disappear.

There are no cats left in
Leningrad. Some dogs are sausage,
some stew. All the men away
at the front the trolley tracks
run to—but no trains run.
My daily slice has sawdust filler.
Chewing on wood, on leather,

I think of caviar, those salt-sweet
jellies, but this girl's belly holds

only the melted snow
I tease the gnawing hours with.
Forget the noise and smoke—as if
everything you couldn't eat
had turned combustible—compared

with starving, bombs are
just a joke. What poet said
history is sister to hysteria?
Thank God, Mother will never see
what happens next. Oh, Grief's a
baby! I saw him in the night. He was
all white, his arms up over his head

in panic, as if he couldn't breathe.
And as I reached to help
he fell down dead. Last January I
refused to pull my brother
on his sled. Now there's no
reason to refuse. One by one
I've watched the others go.

The roads are rutted, trees on
either side, white and fruitless.
Coming out of town, I saw a hill.
Closer—a leg cut off at the knee,
some frosted hair. It was a mountain
of bodies jutting into the sky.
Thousands strewn around the cemetery

gate, no one strong enough to hack
their holes in the frigid ground.
So many deaths can hardly be
serious! And now, tottering back,
I watch the others—those exhausted,
dutiful faces—shoving coffins,
dragging shrouded sleds, stumbling,

weak like me. One of them dropped
in the snow: pale blue skin
over the bones of her cheek.
And gazing into her beautiful
green glazed eyes, like shells,
there is no way to tell
which of us is living, which dead.

While the Pope and the President Meet at the Fairbanks Airport, the Poet Takes a Walk

Before the invention of eyes
only the nearness of things
counted. I walk down Rosie Creek

Road, and imagine the little
neon airport lounge you
are having a glass of sherry or

port in. Sitting across a knee-high
table on plastic upholstery—
"And how was China, Mister

President?"—you come from
far corners and bless
the permeable conditions

which light throws out like jacks.
The ice on the Tanana's all gone
gray, the road is mud

despite the best efforts of
our local road committee. In China they
build walls, Rome's aqueducts

crumble in polluted air. Once
in St. Peter's Square my father
lost a watch. But none of that

seems to matter. In the circular
drift of my thought, I'm
proceeding quite well on my walk.

Stunned by the loud *thwop-thwop*
of a copter bouncing off the ridge
the dogs speak up for spring,

hating their chains. It's a bit
like war and peace meeting in
Fairbanks. Once when I was a kid,

Kennedy came to speak at the town
depot, a speech that was dead
on his lips. After that I didn't

go in for current events; instead
I speak for the greater ir-
relevancies. The impudent pasqueflower

knows what it thinks. It's a permanent
resident. The rest are passing through.
Hard to imagine dialogue for you,

a conversation between costumes.
But I bet there are smiles,
flashbulbs, a bunch of important

aides talking on walkie-talkies.
Is one of them phoning out
for pizza? Well, gentlemen,

you are welcome to Fairbanks
where juncos and chickadees flit
and flirt, the key is in the lock

and turning, and the warming river
loosens its thigh under
            flashing intermittent sun.

   May 2, 1984

Pictures of the Dead

The dead have no location, no language.
They do not gossip.

When you join the dead they will not
welcome you into their club.

The dead ear does not hear the dirge.
It is not deaf.

The population of the dead is zero.
A massacre in Corsica will not add to their numbers.

A dead babe does not age in the grave.
It does not stay young either.

If you are feeling sorry for yourself,
you are still alive.

The pictures we have of the dead are not accurate.
The flowers are appreciated.

Walking Past Midnight

for Linda Schandelmeier

Dusk in the arctic whistled me
out of bed. I felt its feathers
brushing by. Moon pink in the west;

a solitaire's call, a thrush.
I saw a rabbit freeze on the road,
heard a dog-pack howling. I love

the motion and the smell of spruce,
but this is not a walk that
gives much pleasure. My thoughts keep

straying back to what you said
about your baby's whimpers—like a
damaged animal's . . . and when her doctor cut

to find the elusive vein, you had to
flee the room. Then, as they rushed her
down the hall in shock, the pain

it gave you fevers in my mind:
meningitis. Deep in the bloodstream
one black ship's enough. Mild

fermentation in the air. This is
the light that leaks across the pole
at two A.M. in June, a watery light.

I dip below and bring up bits of
childhood like small fish the great
whales herd, and harvest with a blow.

And from the other side of life's

division, I think of Jeffrey's pride at
four, leaping from a seawall to the beach

while I stood by and watched him
break his collarbone. At the bottom
of the hill I turn and for a while

tilt with the body's knowledge
of its route. . . . They flushed your
baby's blood with bottled blood and

sat with you the night. Now Mara's
home, her head of rough black hair,
round face and active eyes. Deprived

of your bereavement, teasing death
holds his mirror up to nothing
and is gone. Another thrush

trills bravely to the dawn. Stiffly
the rabbit stood as I approached,
then dashed into the woods.

Sitting on a Wasp

We're always leaving the summers
behind: remember Dickinson,
ND, where you spent a whole

week once digging bones on the
brown plateau? The DC-3
that bounced you out from Minnesota

carried Miss North Dakota too.
And in the little western town, the mayor
and councilmen were waiting at

the airport. It was 'an event,'
one of the few you've been an in-
cidental part of. Of course they forgot

to unload your bags, distracted by Miss North
Dakota, who also distracted you
from remembering to be sure. It was

the way she occupied her body,
knowing she was a very special package
and had to be handled with care.

Remember, they carried a parasol
to shield her from the sun, and sun
was everywhere. That summer the surface

of the earth seemed special too,
oil wells plumbed its magic
fluids, rattlesnakes like jeweled

necklaces slept beneath stones.
The wasp was long and thin and black,
a sharp machine. Pain made you dance.

We're always about to sit on an
accident, the sting of chance,
which like the suddenness of beauty
can only happen once. And once. And once.

The Wreck

Clinging to branches and roots, I scramble
down from the road, boots filling with loose gravel.
Every inch a dent, its blue gone gray—
this beauty that someone I'll never know drove
over the edge. A spidery rooflight dangles from its wires.
And under the hood, everything useful to man
has been removed. The lower door hangs slack,
where the victim, I suppose, crawled out.
Some moss, a lovely green, fills up the driver's seat.

       * * *

An emergency of rosehips, fireweed,
and aspen. In the half-light of midnight,
she lost the wheel and spun out
down the slope, snapping a dozen
branches—loud as pistols—off,
tumbling over trunks. Brief takes
of pain scut through like mice.

Where was she going when falling
intervened—another brutal marriage,
some darker bar? Her griefs,
a chain of bullets strung about
the neck—as the battered blue Corolla
thuds against a final spruce,
she feels the scald of what they'll say,

her cousins back in Ruby. The windshield's
flaring sunburst splinters into her head.
She wonders are those brains or rapid clots
that dribble down her arms, dark red.
After such whirling: stillness. The hill

behind's unclimbable, each breath's a flame.
Why had it seemed so important to hold the road?

* * *

The high hawk rides on harshness. He cannot see her heart.
Too soon, she thinks, a dog-faced cop will pull her free
and run her in. As she dozes, the shards of glass dissolve.
She's with the hawk. Above the river's silted gold,
she watches the forest fold around the car:
willow bush and birch; dead leaves sift in. Her own decay
is sudden. Ants tunnel through nostrils and ears. Gnats
drink out her eyes. And when her old shirt shreds, cracked
ribs poke through. Below, the rapid river tumbles, shining.

Crossing the Rhine

Within the metal girders of the bridge
enemy fire rattled and ricocheted.

No angle was safe, your leg could be
ripped from behind, your belly gutted.

Our own troops tried to cover us,
but shells came down from the hills

and we were open. My thoughts moved
out of history like a bug on a rope.

The crossing was not of water
or of air. Some hostile element

beat down on us—I don't mean gas—
and seemed to constrain our joints.

Dashing from girder to girder, taking
what cover there was and taking fire,

the morning grew white. A mile and a quarter
of flak. We left the groaners twisting,

slowly dying. In battle first things first,
even your friend: not that you care for him

less, a bullet in his neck or shrapnel,
trying to stanch the spurt. And I thought

of the other world—you couldn't help it

there in the heat. It seemed real close.

And once I glanced at the river
and saw the shadow of the bridge,

a bold invention, steady on the flow.

Approaching the Whitestone Bridge

Cables, arches, piers—there are more parts
to a bridge than he can name. Beyond,
Shea Stadium, LaGuardia, and thousands
of ordered homes that fade toward the sand.
His parents, both retired; now their occluded
talk draws a limit to thought at the waterline.

A splotched gull leaves its perch and
loops down toward a scow. Why should a tomb
be only for the dead? Part of him still
wants to live with the force that can shape
a beautiful line flexing over the water.
He sees it next to him—her arm on the sheet

last night as he put his book on the stand,
reached across her and pressed out the light.
In darkness, there were sparks, the purified
gists of sunlight and now it continues
to spread and smells like a field after burning.
Once, going out of Egypt, there were so many

weeks of stone before you came to the hills.
At such times he feels each detail needs
attention, in case some god should look in.
A few high, pungent clouds, and the delicate
scent of gas. And what the eye holds vast
might just as well be small—a sphinx a scarab,

or the red clay head of a Nubian girl
no bigger than a wasp. The tiny dental mirror
reflected her long, thin braid, painted on behind.
Cutting his own son's hair, in a moment's
carelessness, the scissors nicked an ear, as if
to say: this one is mine. Not far from here

his reticent father showed him the heavy spin
on a left-handed curve. And earlier still
he'd crouch by the radio, unwilling almost
to breathe, knowing the slightest move could
shift the play-by-play. He thought his will
connected to each pitch and sometimes his

giddy prayers had bite. Morning rush hour
past; to the west, those shadowy towers:
how many intangible teeth? Now he rarely looks
at a box score. His folks, expecting him
in Queens—will he be articulate today?
He smiles, almost hears himself say,

"Let us consider the heart, whose hidden
fifth chamber holds the shadow of a bird,
spread on a satin napkin like a stain."
He drops exact change in, recalling an
earlier fear: that this drive ends mid-deck
in a jagged fall. Less fragile now, he

senses the other shore. But when someday
a stone is rolled before the tomb?
Air traffic flows, the nights resume
their walk. In ages of decay, perhaps
some bluish afterglow remains, in spite
of dreams still faithful to this world.

Letter from the Camp: the Pearl Fishers

Because we'd given in
to almost everything, our ranks
dissolve, sky-writing in a high mist.
Too skinny for games or laughter
we choke on the speckled air, tubercular,
as ghostly Mozart wafts
over the camp like mustard gas.

Oh, for a secret passage
out of the accumulated future of the race.
Recall Berlin, ten years ago
in subterranean light, two pearl fishers hung
among the pasty coral. Soft
in our bones we watched
through air

another world where lungs
are wasted—the fishes
still, suspended—
hearing as if in some third ear
waves breaking like stones
on a far shore, the tumble
of birth, the infinite suck of the sea.

The Inside Passage

Pink and azure like the common jewels
in our original nudity we
slip through, the mill all white
and wonderful beyond this dusk.

Pear-scented grasses in easy profusion
bloom, as if all out of doors
were happening in this room where
the masters of diction suggest alternatives.

Is this the exile we hoped for
when we whispered together? Hands
big as pitchforks perfecting
this blood on its leash between hairs.

And having forgotten already
the color of our fear, we retire
our bodies in tandem, aligning their parts.
How calmly each bud unpuckers

like a child's pale tongue receiving
a wafer of light. These arts
outstrip our caution because
they are needful and free. Such

commotion, so mild! Scattering leaves
we bury the oldest of bones.
So in your dream a ship
with orange burning oars—Assyrian,

Greek?—rowing away to the north
discovers a passage unbounded
by flesh where our savior is ravishing
both ends of the earth.

II

Above the Tanana

The Tanana River rises in the western Yukon
Territory and flows northwest for about
eight hundred miles across interior Alaska before
joining the Yukon. The setting of this sequence is a ledge
overlooking the river, near Fairbanks, Alaska,
with a long view south to the Alaska Range.

Above the Tanana

January: *for William Stafford*

The first returns of light at ten A.M.—pale
strips of salmon colored cloth sewn

to high clouds, in hazy silhouette
the distant range. I look down

on the river stalled with ice. The other day
a fog bank sat here like a blank gray wall.

The airport closed. And I myself had stalled,
voiceless in the cold. *The world,* you wrote,

will give and give. I know it takes back too.
But now the lengthy dark begins to lift.

Last night I dreamt I'd built a wooden platform
on this ledge. A thousand friends

and faces that I've known all crowded in
—and you among them, Bill—to share

the view. With animation, fingers pointing,
we agreed, we disagreed by turns, I had my say—

a righteous gathering. And even now I'm
not alone. Two shrill squirrels chitter back

and forth below me from the tops of nearby spruce.
What voice I have is partly theirs. In growing

light—the tracks of skis and snow-machines.
I scan for moose and feel the space,

a fourth dimension opening me up, as if a man
could blossom to himself in such a place.

The first low sun's bright orange seed
pierces a V-shaped cleft beside Mt. Hayes

and picks me out. My dream was laced
with friendly argument that proved

the flow of everything toward light.

February: *for the Kahn-Morgan Social Club, 1945-48*

I've climbed down here again and everything's
changed—a quilt of gray covers the flats.

A hundred miles south the sharp peaks float
in massive disconnection from the land.

It looks like you could sail a ship beneath them.
Out skiing on the river yesterday, I skirted

domes and cracks of shifted ice, as slanting
flurries tapped against my goggles, and looking

toward this ledge I thought I saw
my absence, staring at the skier down below.

Kid snow-machiners, masked like aliens,
looped by—and then my glide began to slow

where water seeping through an open lead
had turned the trail to sludge, caking my skis.

I knelt and snapped them off. And, walking, I remembered
Rockaway, the winter I was three and had the mumps—

snow filling up the yard above my chin.
While all four older cousins in our house

were sent two miles or more through mounting drifts
to scout up some 'essentials' at the store,

I fogged the window, watching jealously,
until at last my eye was taken by those

countless flakes of darkness in the sky,
that sifting downward lifted up the yard

turning it white. At five we moved away.
I saw my cousins rarely then and learned

the artifice that knits up separations. A mind
must travel far to find its home. Still,

when snow comes down, though forty-one,
I'm waiting for my cousins in that storm.

March: *for Arthur Morgan*

Squinting at the glare of melted and
refreezing slush—the ice-thick river fierce

with sun—I see through haze the hospital's
white room, your arms extruding bright machinery,

your mind in partial ruin. Mother gripped
the phone and calmed her voice: "Your father's

had a stroke." You've lost the names
and call the pen they hold up "something

that you write with," and the watch
"a thing for telling time." I shut my eyes,

reaching for what it means to be in love
with words and have them blotted out.

I understand your anger. Strange what time will
bury and exhume: when I was sick I used to think

my feet were mountains down at the horizon
of the bed. You were one peak, mother

was the other, and the sheet flowed like a
glacier; its whiteness soothed my fever.

Below me on the river, a black setter drags
a toddler on her orange sled. A woman jogs behind.

I break a chip of spruce-bark, smell its resin
and recall Muir Woods—the green enormous shade—

which we visited last Christmas. Ben
led the way—"C'mon, Artie!"—half a mile up

a side trail till we turned him. You were
having trouble breathing. Now I sit here

stung by whiteness, going over mother's words.
"The doctors think it's hopeful; there's

no leakage to the brain." We left out
"death" and rushed on to "recover," but a wind

comes off the river: I hug myself,
I shiver, and my lungs

are short of breath.

April: *for the New Rochelle High Class of '61*

A crane, in snow showers, drifts above the river
where, this morning, two jet fighters buzzed

the flats. I look for other signs of life.
A scrap of blue-green color on the ground

turns out to be the wrapper of a half-inch
firecracker. Did Jeffrey—ten next Thursday—

set it off? Last fall (as thought steps back)
at our 25th reunion, Molly, now a writer of romances,

seemed old in flashy makeup and long lashes.
We danced in the 9th grade to Buddy Holly

holding close, and once, in nursery school
as I recall, we shed our underpants

to have a look. Now "Muzzy" (John Mazzulo)
is a medical professor, adamantly gay.

And most bizarre—John Seaman, our
annual class president, still "a real

nice guy," has made himself a star
in porno flicks. But look at me. With hair

down to my shoulders, back East from far
Alaska and a poet—I'm one of the exotics

of the class. We sat on the grass beside
the whitewashed Tom Paine Cottage—kept

as it was by those radical D.A.R.s—and talked
about the ones who weren't there. Steph,

my hopeless crush in the third grade,
dead of a brutal tumor these ten years,

and Andy Miller, 6-2 white point guard, who
turned to drugs and dealing, and got blown away.

I said we'd put on masks: balding, gray,
and wrinkled "monster" versions of ourselves.

And now banning that thought, knitting
my brows, I spot a spider netting two

spruce bows. What's near at hand grows deeper
in the evening light. Beyond her web

the mountains darken under storms. A crescent moon
flies suddenly among the splotchy clouds. The river's

mud-green current swells under thinning ice.

May: *for Nancy*

Here are the pasques, those
purple-arising, yellow-hearted flowers

brave as spring. And far below,
a duck, small bursts of wing-power

motoring along. Perched on a root above
the slough, we watch the melt of ice

flow west, a tent of wood that piles
on a bar, a dark bird looping lark-like

down—so artless, unintended
like that kiss to which our lips

were given twenty years ago. There
on the banks of an urban river

I fixed you in my heart and you
were young as tenderness itself.

A raven passing overhead: he chortles,
caws, and sings, coaxing his mate

along. I add them to my list. Birds
to what purpose? Seeds of a garden

rooted in the mind. I knew when I
first saw you, I could outwait the facts.

Now, where mountains, sharp and white,
are rimmed with sky, where river ripples

stipple dark and light, here on this
shelf—hushed, we can almost hear

the tune the earth is singing to itself.

June: *for Ben and Jeffrey*

Slaps of a paddle and the rambling
drone of *Discovery's* guiding voice

through a microphone (stern-wheeler crammed
with tourists small as ants) carry

up to us across the sweet and
treacherous Tanana, river cold with

glacial melt, whose banks we've
climbed from. "And here's an anthill, Jeffrey"—

Ben points down, loving the little
like his own. We settle on the

roots of a forward spruce. I show them
tiny petals of blue vetch. Not

far from here last summer a
nameless teenager launched his car

off a ledge full-speed and
looped into the depths, with no

trace found. Worried about edges,
I take Ben's hand. Jeffrey at ten

will have to fend for himself
soon. He points out the brilliant red

of a wild rose bud, can't believe these
faded petals are the same. A freaked-

out squirrel chitters, drumming, just above
our heads, then dashes up the trunk—high

comedy—while Jeffrey counts the measures of
a haiku he will enter at the Fair:

> *Branches hanging down*
> *Whistle in the breezy air.*
> *Winter is coming.*

July: *for John Hildebrand*

The wind is up, the cottony seeds
of poplars ride the blow. The river's

full of life—salmon, burbots,
and beavers near the shore. Seagulls

float above and call. Last year you
sat here too and said, "The river's

the old road—the only way to go."
We talked about your boat, your

thousand-mile journey to the coast.
The water moves against the wind,

its motion giving access to
new thought. Is that black thing a log

or what—poking around across the way
where smoke angles from a fish-camp tent

like scented silver spray. Alone
I find I've spread like smoke.

Hurried here and there among the fertile
trees, mosquitoes shun me. How close am I

to grace (I ask) and then recall
I'm forty-two this month, halfway to

hell and gone. Still, what's another year?
I'm always different but the same.

You built a cabin once, hoping to find
a life, and found your separate

loneliness instead, when your first child
died. Ah, John, I've built here too,

five thousand miles from my youth.
Each journey circles round some

absent truth. Meanwhile, I'm going
no place in this snow of seeds,

finished with one more year, one
half a life, and starting out again.

August: *for Bill and Tina*

Brown river, muddy and high, braiding
through islands, weaves out of the east

heavy with smoke. A fishwheel combs
the farther shore; the season's in decline.

Good friends who built our house,
in the sudden bust of the oil

economy are trucking out. We've watched them
frame a cabin on the back of their Chevy pickup,

load the family in and sway off south.
The nameless goldfish stays with us. Also

the unloadable canoe. Alone on this
companionable root I watch my thoughts

flare into rhyme, as if the Tanana touched me off.
Loud buzz of a fireplane draws my eye through

layered greens. I think of that laborious
acrobat Monet and wrestle with my focus

on the way the smoky light flattens
distant trees to strokes of gray. Beside

my feet, a dragonfly drops to the sawdust
some busy ants have mined from this aging spruce.

Imagine the labyrinth I crouch above,
like a curious but unhelpful deity.

I hear the slap of a beaver, busy on the slough.
Wood smoke's a sour sauce. It's temporary here.

While fires prowl the edge of town, our banks
go broke in empty malls. An antique four-prop

circles into view, then tunnels into smoke.

September: *for Robert Lowell*

The mountains, Deborah, Hess and Hayes,
like ghosts, step forward in white, recede

in angled grays. And thirty degrees from
south, a rainbow hangs a fickle swatch

above a stand of yellowed birch.
Aspen and birch still hold their leaves,

and every now and then a noisy motorboat
comes in, crushing its predecessor's waves.

The slough's low shine gives some of
this picture back—inverting trees and sky.

If art were simply mirroring,
I'm sure it does a better job than I. Alone

at early dusk with a last mosquito or two,
and one chilled, unexpected grasshopper,

my thoughts jump back to you—a rangy master,
making the commonplace and the uncommon

heart speak out in that adopted urbane
southern voice. Among the cautious intellects

at Harvard, you stood for something else.
I see your big hands shaping space,

your index finger stirring an imaginary cup,
and for a moment I can feel your crazy weight

lounging here beside me on this shelf. What
would you make of this jigsaw-puzzle picture

time and place: the river's autumn sweep,
so wide and low (the gulls and geese have left)

with dark gray sandy bars a few days shy of snow.
Great cloud-decked sky whose arch includes

a horse's mane, dark stippled fish, and
the charcoaled muscles of an open heart.

October: *for Jerry Cable*

The trees are softened by a touch of snow
that cottons what was harsh a day ago. I tune

my ear to the riffles where the river
tumbles in the slough and hear dim music.

Against the view, I see your bearded face
gone gray and hear your heavy breathing

as the sleep-gas takes effect. Today
the men who couldn't solve your pain

last spring will cut again. Christ,
thirty pounds ago they made you give up drink!

Now I begin to shiver, stand and jog in place,
keeping a distance from the edge. Old friend,

we've lost our summer tans. Sometimes I curse
the bland miscalculations of our lives . . .

      * * *

—Next day; skim-ice on the slough,
and floating down the river thousands of

growing shapes, each roughened with a three-inch
pelt of snow. An Africa drifts by me,

a Japan—these puzzle pieces merged of ice and mind—
whales and raccoons, a ferret and a shark.

And the magnified shape of something worse.
They sliced you open yesterday, and found

a tiny ice-boat aiming its malignant
cold harpoon—and then they closed you up.

Your new face floats before me,
one of the presences the river bears:

like souls, I think, that gather in the mountains
and raft to the Bering Sea. Or those intriguing

oddballs, Jerry, who ride your poems,
breathing the sharp impression of your

feeling art. But when the ice floe stalls,
and winter saps the earth's robust physique . . . ?

This goes beyond my competence to speak.

November: *for Muriel Morgan*

White dunes, the sifting ash of snow.
Bright burnished metal saucepan sun, hung

low to my right—so alien it might not
be our star. On this uninhabitable outer world

drier than Mars, I've made a ladder of logs
and climbed down to my spot, exposed

to the wind and view. It's ten below,
but under the ice a rush of water, heard . . .

then lost in the sudden shaking roar
of a jet, braking on a runway—taking off?—

six miles from here. Suppose I strip
myself bare—unzip my parka, snap off

this sheepskin vest, down to the long-johns
underneath, in homage to the cold, to make

it speak. Out of my throat a forcing shout
carries from the center of my lungs

and you could count the miles, count
the years that voice has traveled from its first

intrepid screaming as your doctor dreamed me forth.
Mom, you wouldn't like it here. Too much

of cold, of space, of the meandering,
ice-paved river. You prefer right angles

and ("once you've seen a mountain or a moose . . .")
you are a generalist, get lost in the

particulars of place. A patch of orange fog
above an open lead. That mystic pinkish glow

below the range, as in a painting by O'Keeffe.
I sit before this canvas, slowly baking

into what I was, a city boy before a window, gazing
into snow as warmed imagination washes out my grief.

December: *for Spirit*

Toward the end of the year—perhaps
this is always the case—I'm

looking for a sign. The mountains, like a
massive wave, rush upon the land.

And striking from below the southwest flange,
sunlight flames the upper sky. Darkness

flows from the east at three in the afternoon.
This month, except for bombs and

hijacked planes, I'd be in Israel.
Is one place better than the next?

Like minor stars three snow-machines
approach downriver with swift, silent speed.

We've trotted to the slough and back.
Overdressed, in double-insulated mittens

and down pants, I watch you chew the snow,
wearing the comfortable hair of a dog.

Hot breath fogs my glasses, while you
nip a thorny branch whose brittle

bract enfolds the rose. In sixteenth-century
Palestine, young rabbis paced the graveyards

of the ancient Torah-tellers, smelt the tar-smell
of redemption burning in their templed hearts.

They knew, no less than Christians do,
this world must be remade. Is it

too late? The other night, at twenty-eight below,
a green aurora branched across the sky.

I watched the sickle moon dip toward
the range. Orion bristled overhead,

jeweled sword, and golden belt of stars:
his state was all the wide and snowy west.

Now that the year is almost dead, have I
done what I set out to do? How have I changed?

At four, the evening star shines through,
the southwest rim is still in flames.

III

The Cyclist

The Cyclist

Alaska in those days seemed open-ended.—John Haines

1

A chill summer day, the sky
a varied gray with squalls to the north
and west, as I pedal shifting gears,
watching for glass. A swallow-tail
flirts for a second with the eye,
a runner passes, bare-chested
in green shorts. And in the bushes

beside the road as my bicycle coasts,
the smell of rotting flesh. Objects
and our ideas about the word
grow and decay. One
month from forty; to my right the river
slides its scaly back. "The world
is flat"—such facts for text,

grasped trembling like that aspen
leaf, twisting on a point I can't
connect: as I move among
gusty ghosts, however fast,
I am this single place,
a man on a bike—he goes
and the world stays.

The woman on the back of the bike
is old and brown. Bones
bruise her skin, breasts flap.
The men putting pipe in the ground
watch us go by and make remarks.
We swerve past their yellow hats.
Her skin a drainage map, behind

which a candle burns, she's like
the withering world. "Sun," she says,
"you are lucky to see us; though
each word you speak is light,
we enhance your self-esteem!"
A sore on her lip looks cancerous,
green liquid oozes from one eye;

yet we celebrate the day's
long season of space and tilt. She
whispers a tune to my ear.—*Einstein
was right, touching disturbs.*
We make a formidable team in this
bicycle riding dream: one of
us is wise and one can steer.

Trees fall to the river, the bank
is swept away. A portion of
ego flees the self, lodging in leaf
or fern, in broken glass,
or the flat black ring of a tire
from which a yellow sign ascends,
a warning. Now between me

and the river (I sit at my desk)
orange trucks pass hauling dirt.
A bicycle coasts by, dust rising
scatters. Like an outlaw, the gray
goose guards her nest. The sky
and sea, blue-gray, lie cold and far.
Once, as a child, I sat before

death's elegance—Manet's cold matador,
a decorative stain on his chest.
I knew the insufficiency of prayer.
That liquor fermented from grief

could make you whole again
in your belief—skeptic, come like a
god, an invisible cup in your hands.

What is this stain on the ceiling,
the river over its bank, the
window a blur of water? Some bolt
in the rational world has
given way. Who'll patch the roof,
sandbag the cellar—as if the house
of the self had become

a porous enterprise into which
rain's pious blessings break like a flood.
The wooden walls can't take it.
As soon as stated each meaning
is eclipsed. Is it our sins
we're awash in? Are we cursed?
So little at stake, the language

totters, a tower of blocks
some two-year-old just kicked. Down,
tumbling their unnecessary fall,
the pieces scatter, pieces of
the dawn. Soon birches spark the air
with yellow fire. Robins and flickers
fly, then perch, eye to the receding

storm, and fly again. A morning
fanciful with birds and light
beneath which the river seems
more muscular, swift, as if
its energy fed on light spinning
the world, a ball on a slope, a child
letting go and rolling over and over down.

2

Gravel in a drizzly light
is gray, white, brown, small patches,
ovals of tone that slope away
down the road. Trees shake
their intricate hands, the river
is high, and the islands sink
under the flow and look frail.

The grass on their heads thins out.
Into such landscape the self
drifts like a boat, something of water
though firmer, implausibly buoyant
though sopping. It speaks along
the whitecaps, rowing across the grain.
Almost a still point on the river

for all its bobbing strength. Of little
importance, the self insists
and insists like the mist, it
washes the canvas, can't seem to
abandon its task, the rough
round oar-grips, a sense
of unreachable destination.

Friend, are you aware of the
body's knowledge, how it
longs to encounter air without clothes
or postures? That which the finger
has touched, the buttock
broods on. Toes in the sand have to
learn their way down to the colder mud.

Meanwhile the skin of the knee
cocks an ear to the waves, and the
shy armpit shades itself

44

from the sun. Even the hairs
are sniffing. This is the body's way
which the mind, like a finch
in a mirrored cage, envies in its song.

What is a man to do who
sets out with infinite patience
to make a tree: skill shows
in the nailing, the placement and
taping, the shingly texture like scales—
how leaf attaches to stem and stem
to bough at a swivel-point, so that

in the wind it dartles, sharp-edged,
autumnal, and knows the moment
precisely to let go. Once God himself
was a tree, the universe shook
in the wind, all its souls swept away
like blown leaves. Starting over,
perhaps any color will do—a Rothko

blue, or the red of the flag when you
stare close up at a single stripe. The
more you look, the nothing of it grows:
a road without grade, a Moebius strip
of light, monotony of the infinite One
that trembles at the edge of a
leaf, wishing devoutly to fall.

Slicing and patching the canvas
with scissors, placing and pasting
then taking a wash to the whole
to make it even—still
a headline's too black, the
toilet paper wadded. You get a sense
the thing will never work.

In my dream a crocodile rises
from the river. Swans and
geese dash off from his potent
jaws, and I think, "Good reason
to own a gun," bailing
my boat in mid-river
and rowing one-handed for shore.

3

The Tanana weaves among islands
carrying ice, those smaller
islands that float, white
upon gray, shuffling this way
and that as the channels decide.
The spruce, more black than
green, are scruffy silhouettes.

Without sun everything flattens,
a photograph of itself and the texture's
like peppery flakes of snow.
The islands of ice are angels, growing,
the gray sky broods. One morning
the river stops. But the eye
moves over ice expecting motion.

A surface of packed ice, all
mottled white and gray,
but here and there a glassy lead
still shines that could be ice or water.
I notice one thing more: the few
leaves left on an aspen ripple,
butterflies drying their wings.

The sun's a luminous ball
behind the light gray clouds.
In this imperfect stillness life

draws back into itself.
A dusting of snow on the gravel.
A gray car passes. Two ravens pause
then dip below the spruce-line.

Light used me for its purpose, drawing
edges, washing colors into whiteness
but at night a waxing grayness
stole the midnight back, where
in the dark dominion, stars
diagram the sky and meteors by the dozen!
—Too much. The lovers in their cars

lose interest, go back to touching.
The lower branches dead, but up above
a cloud of leaves still pebbles the sky.
Earth-moving trucks carry their proud
loads past. I hear with another ear:
out of the mist, an unearthly crackle
as if the fault line moved again.

Unsteady the rolling earth, but then
two birds, long necked and fat in
the belly float over. One lets out
a honk like a tin can tossed in a pail,
an echo of the laugh in the hollows
of the world when the last lights had
scattered and God sat alone in the ruin.

Under the porch the bicycle hangs
upside down. In snow the prints
of squirrels, dogs. The self,
a bear under a quilt: its breath
is steam, ice forms on its fur.
Driven inside, it has little to say.

Ice on the river thickens, the sun

hangs low, an orange egg, then sinks.
Hourly jets take off for the south.
Standing on earth, I move my hand
through a cloud and shape it. Severe
and retrograde beliefs have called
me home. I live in a hole in a tree,
where love keeps its staggered hours.

By the late sheen of an arctic sky
alive with branches shimmying with
light he comes to me: the cyclist,
active, floating, magical, observant,
and the poem comes from him—
whatever he can make it: the hope
that what he turns to will take hold.

IV

The Third Walk: McKinley Park Hotel to Mt. Healy Overlook

Wind in a bush gives me a start. Moose sign
but no moose, no bear. I whistle a Dvořák
serenade—calm fatalist—against my fear.

Helped by the wind, I rise above willow
and spruce. Bluebells and wild roses lend
their colors to the green. And as I

bend to a monkshood's purple flower,
this thought: somehow before the age of
ten, I let death in. He was a strong

ally. Again and again I penciled
his flag of skulls in my school
notepad. Switchbacks winding me up,

I lean my treacherous balance against
the slope. Red squirrels, marmots—
relative pacifists. And sitting

at the level of a peak, white
snow on charcoal gray, I write this down,
sip from a grapefruit can, and climb again,

straying beyond the trail. On a slope
of scrabbly shale, tilting me back, I cling,
knowing the slightest breeze can

lift me off. I feel like a fool,
light-headed, a leaf, a wing—
among the shattered rock, lost between

here and there, part of me willing to go.
And surfacing from childhood, a small
boy edges across a vertical face,

loses his grip, and falls with the weight
of things on stone. Then, not quite knowing
how, I inch my way back to level ground.

At a rocky overlook, I open a bag
of chips and watch one float away.
Slowly a freight snakes north

through the valley cleft, the river's
foil, a sinuous body of light.
Below, to my left, a toy-like Cessna

plays on the wind; behind, above,
the mountain looming still.

To the Muse

Sitting with your daughter
in the campus bar, your eyes
like wounds, your hair distressed—
I asked if I could join you,
ordered us daiquiris.

And as we talked—the price
of silk, the temperature
in Bangkok—I kept hoping
you'd unbend. My company's
no better than the rest?

Of course I'd heard about
the late divorce, your lover's
cancer, analyst's accident;
how everything's gone, as you said,
"from bad to verse."

(The Muse in our time
is pretty grim.) I'm feeling
like a kid on a first date
with the girl he loves: they sit
on the couch and watch TV.

He doesn't even touch her hand.
I spent an evening once
with such a girl. She
went to Berkeley, had a
nervous breakdown junior year.

Next thing, she was in Thailand
married to a prince.
I felt that she had fled the world,
as if all beauty, gentleness
—whatever can be praised—

had gone kaput. I'm bolder now,
keep up a decent patter—current
flicks, the spin of
antimatter. And so we've
met again, years later

middle aged. You have a daughter,
a divorce, but
nothing in the raw
commotion of the heart
has changed.

A Dirt Road West of Fairbanks

These geometries lack
dimension. What purpose a
road implies
snakes into distance, willows
and dwarf spruce.

A hawk
clutching a vole
and two or three
buntings leave us no room.

My sons asleep in
the back seat . . .
What if the car stalled?
The someone mining
gold ten miles
off is not reflected
in a hundred lakes.

Spinning around
domes,
       dipping
into mudholes, it's
as if we'd
entered a mirror where
absence of grief is the
active principle.
And moving slowly through
it is a terrible
denial you could not
put on canvas.

Gray sun behind
a rolling overcast, a
billion arctic blueberries

impossibly small
and sour. The heart must expand

again and
again or never take
the measure of this place.

The Suppressed

The end of the world again, well
here we are, monks beating on glass
with our bare skulls.

Observe behind glass this delicacy:
girls placing flowers on a grave.
The tears rolling down their cheeks

are little tanks. And all
we can accomplish
is prayer.

Oh history, inelegant stammerer,
do I hear that the nation of my hopes
goes under again?

Osteology of the Ants

Conglomerate over shale, the top
of the butte sloped gently away
to the south. In a slight
depression, two large anthills.
Giving the self up to its images
I raised my pick and swung.

Out of the sun-flooded gap
dozens of black ants stumbled.
Columns of pale yellow workers
ranged from a deeper tunnel. Where
I had come for bone, I found
the crackling otherness of ants.

Beyond, in a rougher, gouged-out
region, oil rigs punch their tubing
into the saleable past. Mountains—
the scaly back of a ponderous
lizard—drag along the horizon. Half
the anthill slumps down in a whisper.

My exhilaration fires the spaces
around the butte. I rush at the second
anthill, shouting and swinging.
Lugging the rice-like eggs of some
future colony, a tribe of nursemaid
ants marches hopefully forth.

And still my bed has dreams:
magnified insects bear huge boulders
deep into cellars. The leathery
eggs of dragons break and splatter.
The soles of my feet are covered
with jellied ants. The end is this:

clouds and a dark reclusive rumbling.
The wilderness acknowledges my fever.
A gust of wind, a dusty, dizzying odor,
as though some impersonal knowledge
has taken possession of me. How long
since these bones crawled backwards

from the sea? Lightning, thunder—as over
that western valley the rain comes down.

USS *Argonaut*

Submarines, at best
an empire sitting room:
brass candle sticks, brass knobs
reflected the chandeliers
which jangled out our deaths.

Sure you imagine it all ten times over
but you can't
know what happens when you
hit bottom like a corpse.
The bottom-dwelling creatures
gather in your palms, thighs, heels,
and suck you into their sea.
Soon a half-mile round
has you as an aura.
          And within months
no square foot of ocean is without you.
You drift like oil
into every port. Far better than dust
is to be lost at sea.

Married

Quakers perform their own marriage, but
I couldn't pass. Your doctor-father
expected at least an Ethical
Culture wedding like his. In the room
your mother'd frantically unchristened
and reupholstered the week before
Christmas, Rabbi Jacob K. Shankman
presides—in the name of Moses and
the God of Israel. Then the champagne—
the old dragon knows his champagne—those
effervescent relatives, and we
pose hand in hand and cutting the cake.

Twenty-nine stories over Central
Park, its skaters, zoo, and holiday
lights, we went to bed early. We're blocked
by pain, fears, fail, wake unresolved
from long dark. Rain on Friday. Look,
down there's the Met; the American
Museum; that's the Delacorte, where
we saw *Love's Labour's Lost* and *Troilus*
last summer, courting, promising.
You've got an art journal to write; I
take in El Greco's vision; love's
uneasy. Night, Christmas Eve, and we

retired early again. Now marriage
makes us, who'd pictured only starry
nights, weep. We hold our bodies, our spirits
brace, but there's a wall between us.
Then between us the tense, immaculate
fear gives way before your love. Your love,
my brightest crescent, Ares am I,
above the city, the world, the dozen

gates of heaven squeak open; angels
cry, carols rise from the ice rink
speakers. We exchange art books, beam, have
breakfast in bed. Christ, I love you, Nancy.

Moo

The calf I held outweighed me
twenty pounds and kicked like a bitch,
and I could tell by his wide
round eyes as they cut
off his balls—hell, he was only a baby!

A potent singe of hair:
when they put the indelible
"S" to his tender buttocks
his body gave forth brute noise.
And love, I thought, might be like this,

the scrotal scars and scalded
rump, pains that could make a man
become a voice. "Moo!" the calf cried,
"Moo, Moo!" as it happens my mother's
name that willows in my blood.

That night in the spruce-wood
dining hall, the bruise on my shin
turning blue hurt plenty. A bunch
of bravos from the coasts, kids
on a lark, so smart-assed and so horny—

clowns, we ate those prairie-oysters fried.

Rembrandt on the Hudson

Bright tulips glimpsed through a
window. A clipper tacks in the dusk.
Paint like revolutions can
disfigure: the subject is darkness
surrounding the figure who holds
the brush, the darkness of
money or the lack thereof,
a waste of power in accumulation.

Looking past the figure, eyes
soft from lack of sleep,
shadows drift like small talk
from a fire burning somewhere else,
perhaps in a winter garden
amid questions of marble shapes.
For Rembrandt is old now
even in his fat biography's

terminal pages. Awkwardly
behind its frame the landscape
of his youth slides by: farms,
a fort by the sea, green gatherings
of spring. Partially mad, he
inhabits a cellar with a tame
lion and goes on with his work,
depicting without grief a windmill

beating time on a final plain,
and inside the windmill
a stranger grinding corn,
a man who plans no more. Once
it was so easy to be personal,
now he wants nothing from life

not readily available to all; done,
he sits on his ox and sways

toward home, an ignorant, happy man.

The Beach Walk at Port Townsend, WA

for Nancy

No walk outlasts its day. Back
of the beach, logs like bones
or pillars, gray from the weather,

and there's an actual pillar
broken among the trunks. Who threw it
down the cliff and why

to be among its brothers? Ferries
ply the strait and sailboats
set their wings against the blue.

Beside me, shards of charcoal
on the beach—another form trees
take—, glass, the dried out skins

of sea anemone. Nature's punning always,
loving the twist of a name. Gulls
dive bombing mussels onto rocks. Crows.

A salmon eaten out, just skin, with vertebrae
exposed and head. Everyone's eating
something. Even trees eat light. Me, sandfleas

devour with aching tiny bites. Kids
in the surf, tossing a ball. The world at
sport under a sky no pillars support.

I came here to think about poems:
which details count? The whole may
be luminous, but broken into parts

which sandgrain, which occasion rends
the heart? When I phoned home today
you said our two-year-old had learned

to fear his shadow on the road. He
stared and stared and wouldn't move.
Then he saw yours. "Everyone has

a shadow," you said, but he insisted
"*Papa!*" thinking it was me. Ivy
on the cliff and a decorated heart:

"I love you, I love . . ." whoever you are.
Last night in a bar, a Frisco woman said
she loved my work, then talked about some

low things she had done. I left her
sitting in a rented car; the wide-eyed
look on her face, like a child left

at home, shadowed my tipsy sleep.
Curse me if I felt virtuous. I know
those California nights get pretty long.

And now I see—trees, fish, the
swarming sandfleas on the beach, we
all are vulnerable. Waves coming

up the sand, I thread the narrowing
space between water and cliff,
using what distance I have from grief

to muse, to hum. My vanishing
sneaker prints record this
lazy afternoon with you, alone.